Usborne First Stories

The Princess and the Pig

Heather Amery

Illustrated by Stephen Cartwright

Language consultant: Betty Root
Series editor: Jenny Tyler

There is a little yellow duck to find on every page.

This is Grey Stone Castle.

This is King Leo and Queen Rose. They have two children called Prince Max and Princess Alice.

Max and Alice are playing in the garden.

They have lots of old clothes for dressing up.
They are pretending to be kings and queens.

"What's that?" asks Alice.

"There's something in that big puddle."
"It's a small pig," says Max. "It can't get out."

Alice picks up the pig.

"Poor little pig," she says. "He must have escaped from the sty. And now he's all muddy and wet."

"Now you are all muddy too," says Max.

"Don't let Queen Mama see you. She told you this morning not to get your dress dirty."

"I'll go indoors," says Alice.

She carries the little pig into the castle. Alice finds a tub and puts the pig in it.

Alice fetches some water.

She goes to the well and fills two buckets with water. Then she carries them back to the castle.

Alice puts the water in the tub.

She finds some soap and a brush. She washes the pig all over. The bubbles make him sneeze.

The pig is very clean now.

Alice lifts him out of the tub. She dries him with a towel. The pig tries to run away.

The Queen comes in.

"Where did you get that pig? And why are you dirty?" she says. "Just look at your dress."

Alice holds up the pig.

"I found him in a puddle," she says. "He's such a pretty pig." She kisses him on his snout.

There is a big flash of light.

"What was that?" asks Alice. She looks at the pig.
He isn't a pig now. He has turned into a prince.

"Can't he stay with us?" says Max.

"No," says the Queen. "We can't have a strange prince in the castle. Change him back at once."

Alice kisses the prince.

There is a flash of light. The prince has turned into a pig again. "That's better," says the Queen.

"Take him back to the sty."

"And don't kiss him again," says the Queen.
"No," says Alice. "I like pigs better than princes."

This edition first published in 2003 by Usborne Publishing Ltd, 83-85 Saffron Hill, London EC1N 8RT, England. www.usborne.com
Copyright © 2003, 1996 Usborne Publishing Ltd.